The Girl Who Left You

After Hours Poetry

by

Amber Decker

𝔗op 𝔖helf 𝔓oetry 𝔖eries #4

After Hours Poetry

The Girl Who Left You
Copyright 2014 © Amber Decker

Top Shelf Poetry Series #4
Six Ft. Swells Press
www.AfterHoursPoetry.com
www.facebook.com/SixFtSwells

Editors: Todd Cirillo; Julie Valin
Cover Photo: Matt Amott
Book & Cover Design: Julie Valin, The Word Boutique,
www.TheWordBoutique.net

Acknowledgements
Bellwether, At 7pm and *Gravity* were previously published in the chapbook, *True North* (Maverick Duck Press, 2013). *At 7pm* first appeared on "Poetry Superhighway."

All rights reserved.
Printed in the United States of America.
No part of this book may be reproduced in any manner without written permission except in the case of brief quotations included in critical essays, reviews and articles.

ISBN 13: 978-0985307530
ISBN 10:   0985307536

for the ones who stole my heart
the ones who broke my heart
and the ones who kept the pieces safe—
I love you

What's Inside

...Intro by Todd Cirillo...	7
Backseat	11
Riptide	13
Cafuné	14
The Moment I Decided Not to Sleep With You	16
Driving Back to West Virginia	17
They Are Burning the Orchards	18
Camouflage	20
Resistance	22
Fearful Symmetry	24
Hunted	26
Bullseye	28
The Quiet He Keeps	29
At 7pm	31
Letting Go	32
Bellwether	34
If You Ever Leave Me, I'll Kill You...	35
Remains	36
Layover, Dallas/Fort Worth	38
Romancing the Astronomer	40
Gravity	42
At the Motel 6	43
Flash Point	44
Summer, One Year Later	46
An Inventory of Lost Things	48
What She Doesn't Know	50
Gathering Storm	52

With Only Her On My Mind

I am stranded in a bar, on an island, waiting for a girl who cancelled. Most of us relate to this situation; on either the stranded side or the one who chose the no-show. So, it makes me laugh and order another round because it is at this moment I begin to write for Amber Decker's book, The Girl Who Left You.

Amber writes with unmasked bravery, a fierceness followed by sexy, followed by sadness and then strength. Poems of Dairy Queens, cornfields, backseats on backroads, the starting of something new and the holding onto what once was. That sound of the first button popping off, the zipper going down and the way the shadows hit the space all around. The reader experiences the first times, last times and one-more times in life with Amber's sometimes brutal but always vivid and true words, which right or wrong, gives us a strange excitement like standing outside as a tremendous storm gathers upon us. The poems give us the back pocket optimism of hope yet the daylight honesty of calling it exactly what it was. This is the deep American beauty of Amber's poetry.

Amber's poems take you back to those moments when your world felt huge and possible yet dressing room intimate at the same time. She presents us with decisions we have all made, that feel like the absolute best decision at the moment, whether it is saying yes or saying goodbye.

The Girl Who Left You is about what happens when someone is gone for good yet stays with you forever...and in poetry as in love, it can't get any better than that.

—Todd Cirillo, poet, editor
8:33p.m. Sandbar, Marco Island, FL

"One morning, about four o'clock, I was driving my car just about as fast as I could. I thought, why am I out this time of night? I was miserable, and it came to me: I'm falling in love with somebody I have no right to fall in love with."

- June Carter Cash

Backseat

We were never romantic
in the classical sense.
Our first time, you pulled off
into a cornfield and we fucked
in the back of your car,
the skin of our knees scraped
red and raw
by the stiff upholstery.
And it *was* fucking, wasn't it?
Fierce and wild and all about
what we wanted,
what we could take
from each other
while the moon laughed
and banged its fists
against the steamed-up windows
like a fat, drunken cowboy.
We ignored it all—
the barking dogs,
the distant crunch of tires on gravel,
the cows lowing in the fields,
the strange, sweet smell of manure.
After, you wrapped me in your t-shirt,
and we laid tangled there
for hours like willow roots.
You said I smelled like gingerbread
and buried your nose in my hair,
and we laughed because it was absurd
and real and funny.

That next morning,
we wore our bruises
proud as prizefighters.
Months later, I carry
the scar of your teeth on my neck,
a small pink flower
buttoned into my flesh.
I like to think it blooms
only at night and smells
something like gingerbread.

Riptide

You beg me
to light fires for you
in the dark cave
where you dwell
between midnight shifts.
Curtains shut
against the prying sun,
we take off our clothes
and let our bodies
guide us through
the maze of shadows,
the spaces between us
thick with smoke,
walls collapsed.
Your fingers
like keys inside me
set off warning bells,
a block-long siren wailing
like a banshee in the dark,
like me when I come with you
on the wide blue island
of your bed.
And you,
a riptide
that drags me deep
into dirty water
and leaves me gasping
for breath,
limbs heavy
with wanting
what it is you give
and especially
what you won't.

Cafuné

> Brazilian Portuguese – untranslatable in English: The act of
> tenderly running one's fingers through a lover's hair

In line at the Dairy Queen, he slides his right hand
into the back pocket of my blue jeans,
a naked gesture of affection, a hard accent
in his quiet language of physical attraction.
The older women nearby roll their eyes
skyward, bejeweled fingers worrying at the buttons
on the collars of their neatly ironed shirts,
and I cannot imagine these women
ever having undressed in front of anyone
or even in front of a mirror. In fact, I wonder
if they are like barbie dolls
with just smooth, sexless dents
tucked between their legs.
Across the street, the bank's electronic sign
proclaims ninety-degrees in bright, pixilated green.
Everything melts in this kind of heat.
In the car, he leans in to lick the last traces of vanilla
ice cream from the corner of my mouth, his hand
kneading its clever way up the inside of my thigh, thumbing
the copper button through its narrow placket,
one finger plucking the black elastic at my hip
like a guitar string, and he sets me swirling
with that single note like a flamenco dancer.
We are young and hopelessly in love
with what our bodies can do for one another.

I spend the cooler, bluer evenings
on the cream-colored loveseat in his living room
trying to write the story of the powerful woman
I want to become, but when I feel the hard heat
of him against my back, and he begins to unlace
the tight coil of my French braid, I know
this is not that story. This is another version
of Sampson and Delilah, a rambling poem about desire
and how his hands in my hair is a thing I want
more than I want to breathe, a weakness
I cannot explain that blooms
like a red flower in the airless space between my ribs,
and I can say that the most beautiful words
I have ever heard are the ones he breathes in my ear
in the middle of the night, and I have never been good
at taking dictation. Something always gets left out,
lost forever in the translation of all the little things
there are still no words for.

The Moment I Decided Not to Sleep With You

In the restaurant, the pink blossoms of the tulips
in the vase on our table hang
heavy as heads at the funeral of a well-loved man.
There are lilacs, purple as an elegant bruise,
braided into your daughter's flaxen hair.
She ignores you, pulls at the tiny silver buttons
at the neck of her dress, crosses and uncrosses her legs.
Light swirls through the beveled glass windows,
a cocktail of colors, airy and transparent
as a bouquet of unkept promises
an absent father makes to his child.
Your blonde wife wears a coat of dark lipstick,
leaves quiet half-moons on napkins, on the curved rim
of her empty wineglass.
She flutters about uncertainly
like a moth at a screen door, begging to enter
the warm, yellow glow of our conversation.
My black dress, the one you say you love best,
matches the color of your fucked-up heart.

Driving Back to West Virginia

I pass through the mouth of the severed mountain.
I am four long hours from the jagged knife's edge
of the nearest coast, pressed into the center
of desolation like a yellow rose between the pages
of *The Scarlet Letter,* unopened since college.
The only lights are the sleepy ghost lights
of interstate towns, motel signs, gas stations, fast food joints
all lit like beacons for the brokenhearted.
I misread *lodging* as *longing,* somehow, and the tall white
letters on the signs at each exit ramp reach out
to curl their long fingers inside of me, to stroke
the place where my heartbeat hammers the blood of fight
or flight into my legs.
They know I am looking for a quick getaway, strategic escape.
They promise to show me things I have never seen:
the houses of dead poets, distilleries, billboards rising
from the gloom to beckon like sailors who have stayed
too long at sea. I have forgotten what it feels like to come home,
the blurry images—him with some other girl bent over
the couch, the look in his eyes when he saw me,
like a man who wakes panicked in the midst of surgery
to the sight of his own chest being sliced into—
are all fading from view like a red harvest moon balanced
on the eastern horizon.
Ahead, a single car trundles along, headlights bouncing
like a lantern
in a wave-tossed rowboat. Inside is a pretty girl
whose slender hands may have undone him, us, easy
as untying a square knot.
And it matters, somehow, so much that I can't breathe,
and the only thing I can hear is the heartbeat sound
the windshield wipers make as they work to sweep back
the scalloped edges of the night and the storm closing in.

They Are Burning the Orchards

I can see the smoke
before I make it out of town,
cross the railroad tracks.
Empty fields spread
toward the 4am horizon
like golden oceans.
The trees have been cut and stacked in piles
as big as houses and set ablaze,
flames spiraling into
the peach-veined morning sky
like signal fires
lit by the survivors of a plane crash
who know with whatever
animal sense still dwells within them
that help will not arrive in time.
Smoke escapes
in great plumes like clouds
of locusts.

After a homecoming dance one year,
a boy and I laid out a blanket
beneath the trees, the air around us thick
with apple scent as he kissed me,
fingers playing at the thin seams of my dress,
and I thought this would be the night
I discovered what it was like
to breathe with the weight
of a whole other person
balanced on top of me. Instead,
we drank sweet tea spiked with bourbon
stolen from his parent's liquor cabinet
he poured from a thermos
into two mason jars, and later,

he held my hand as we walked
to the car, the rolled-up blanket
thrown over his shoulder
like a map of the uncut world
neither of us were ready to explore.

In the coming months, there will be no
fruit left to fill the humid nights
with its bitter sweetness, only
pillared white houses and pavement,
the smooth fingers of lined roads
tearing their way into the green flesh
of the countryside.
Porch lights will stamp out the stars,
bit by bit, and children will wait for school buses
on the corners of streets with names like
Apple Court or Orchard Drive.
One day, my mother will say things like
Do you remember the trees?
And I will just breathe silently
and think of fire and the solid burn
of whiskey, the way it blazed
an unmarked trail
down the back of my throat.

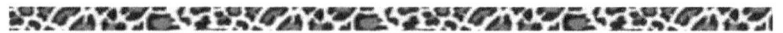

Camouflage

Funny, the way I spoke so honestly with you
about sleeping with your friend
while you pumped gas at the Circle K.

Lights on, no makeup, I waited to be surprised.
Was left waiting.

Gun-shy, I was never out hunting for love.

When the mask dropped, I was not ready
for the camera flash, the ugly parts of me
displayed, no filter, on the other side.

We sat on your tailgate by the river
for hours, shoulders brushing,
until daylight sent me sprinting
back into the shadows of sleep.

In dreams, pillars of fire and smoke.
There was no up or down,
only that directionless heat
hemming me in, smothering.

I had never paid much attention before
to the impossible length of your eyelashes,
the pale sweep of your gaze.

You're beautiful, you said
like it was a gospel truth, irrefutable,
when I caught you staring at me
the same way I stare at sunsets
or wild animals.

Your heartbeat: thunder.
Clouds moving in, dark and sweet enough
to steal my good sense.
My mother's warnings, a distant echo
like dove song tucked into the wind.

Stay low. Seek shelter.
Never trust a stranger's hand.
Be careful who you love.

Even your voice soaked me like rain.

The little girl in me thrilled
at the thought of kissing open your wounds,
stealing the polished jewel of your fear,
sucking it right out of you.

By August, we were tangled up
in that tent by the lake, lanterns
painting our portrait on the nylon
in flickering strokes.

Tucked against your chest, it took hours
for me to fall asleep, so afraid
I would wake in flames
or as ash in a blue dish at your feet.

Hush, you whispered
like a shepherd to his flock
on a full-moon night.

Or the wolf, under his breath, who answers
I'm here. I'm here.

Resistance

Still missing,
I ask after him, knowing
that the words I am offered
from the lips of others
will never take the shapes I desire.
I am a stranger in the halls of sleep.
His side of the bed
grows cold and begins to lose
the shape of him.
My hands have known
the continent of his skin,
his faults and tremors.
I never needed a map, but
I fear I have lost myself,
and there is only
radio silence,
as loud and painful
as the voice of God.
We are no longer allies
in this war against ourselves.
It was never an invasion.
I tell you, in fact, that the enemy
was inside of me,
more than once.
I wanted to believe I was unconquerable.
But I have placed myself at his feet
like a wounded soldier, begging mercy.
They say there are no atheists
in the trenches, and I believe them.
This is not the first time
he has drawn the names
of deities from my lips.

Even the beaches, washed clean each day
by the tides, remain littered
with ghosts, the skeletal fingertips
of ebbing light from the west.
Sleep never comes soon enough
to those who suffer
in the arms of the ones
they do not love.
And these things, too, shall pass,
but storms still come to stir the sea
like a cauldron in the night.
Nothing settles.

Fearful Symmetry

Our town is a small jungle where rumors travel
faster than the sound of danger on the wind.
Intruder, it says.
You don't belong here.
I have heard the whispers, the way the young men lean
into one another with bent elbows,
the flick of their tongues when they speak of her.
Outsider.
The girl with the accent no one can quite place.
She wears her wildness like a perfect coat of lipstick,
her leopard-spotted sunglasses nestled in the blonde coils
of her hair.
In the tavern parking lot, the women huddle like lionesses
in the shade, teeth bared in the bald summer heat as they watch
the smooth glide of her hips, the sun-kissed savannahs
of her bare, tan limbs thick as antelope
as she slides into the leather seat
of her slick mustang GT, the soft, hilly plains
of her gunning by at 90 miles per hour, engine roaring.
We are a tribe.
The women watch her disappear
into the flower of the fading sun. They gossip and smoke
cheap cigarettes, leave red smears on the filters,
cross and uncross their arms like tired housewives
and laugh, mumble things like "whore."
The men have all gone hunting.
We are a tribe, and she
is the tiger spirit who lures husbands into
the trees, spits out the naked mess of their bones
on their widows' doorsteps.

The women cluster around me, hem me in
like a lamb in a pen. To them, I am no longer a threat.
We are a tribe; they want to hear their priestess speak.
They bare the long, white columns of their throats to me,
pass me the ceremonial knife of shame.
But I am not without sin, so I say nothing.
I hold my stones in cupped palms, feel their edges dig
into the soft bellies of the choices I've made,
the consequences etched there,
head line, heart line.
I could split the world in two
with what I know. Once, I took a lover
to the river, allowed myself to be shattered against
the rocks like a golden mirror, like the gates of Troy.
This woman's husband, that one's son
burning bright as the north star.
Somewhere in the tangled night, the tiger slumbers
with my blood and a smile on his lips.

Hunted

The liquor store in Park Circle
has changed hands and names a hundred times,
but it still looks the same on the inside,
dark bottles lining the walls in wire racks,
tequila and whiskey, coolers of beer
in the back so cold that the doors fog
while I'm reaching for what I want—
forty-ounce bottle, domestic,
nothing special. You're paying
for a couple cans of Copenhagen
Wintergreen when I come up front.
Because the clerk knows who you are,
he doesn't ask for your ID or even care
that you are still too young to be
hanging out in liquor stores.
Brown bags in hand, we walk
the two blocks to City Park, settle
onto a wooden bench next to the playground.
Little girls dressed in all shades of pink
are gathered by the swings, propped up
on their skinny, tan legs like flamingos
watching three boys, blonde and bold as lions,
yell and run circles around each other,
arms spread wide in the halos of sunshine
that filter through the poplars.
In a town this small, they will grow up
to be kings. The girls know it and I think
maybe you do, too, as you pack your cheek
then turn to look at me with that crooked
grin you're so good at slipping on and off
for the right girl, like a wedding ring.

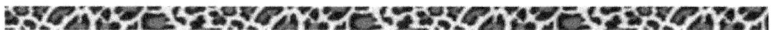

You reach out, slide your left hand
under the hem of my t-shirt,
fingers splayed just over the cave
of my navel, tracing the subtle
black lines of the tattoo that circles it.
Then you lean over, like a tower in slow collapse,
its edges melting toward the pull of the horizon,
and I can feel your heavy breath stirring
the small hairs at the nape of my neck. You say,
"Someday, I'll knock you up,"
then laugh and bite my neck
in a way that feels nothing like being desired
and everything like being marked
as territory or as prey for later
to be
hunted,
eaten,
swallowed whole.

Bullseye

Just after 2am, he pulls his pickup
into the gravel lot of the old lockhouse.
It is a cold night, full of superstitious talk,
black cats and a full moon beginning to sink
full-bellied, down into the river.
A werewolf moon, I say.
His grin is a flash of primal fire in the dark.
Somewhere deep inside me,
something hungry wakens
and shifts, uncurls its insatiable tongue.
We begin to discuss the impossibility
of silver bullets, how they are too light
to be shot accurately at much of anything.
His fingertips brush my knee
as he reaches across to switch off the radio.
I grab his hand, press it to the slope
of my chest where my heart beats
a wild tattoo against his palm.
Don't stop, I beg.
Surprised, he was sure he'd need
more ammunition.

The Quiet He Keeps

Silence is also speech. - Japanese proverb

The boy who rarely smiles
is still beautiful
and heart-breaking
in the mornings, when he wakes
and swings his legs over the side of the bed,
the muscles in his back rippling
like water over rock in the creek
that runs for miles behind his house.
There is something pure
about the quiet he keeps,
about the way he knows that words
are at once holy and terrifying.
Like silence or death.
In the car, I snap a photo of us
to remind myself that this bright world
is just as real and sweet
as Neruda's heart moving through
its tunnel in darkness, as the
sparrow that shattered
itself against the sliding glass door.
Bless him; he knows without asking
how I take my coffee:
no cream, no sugar—bitter,
black as Johnny Cash twanging
through the speakers at our feet.

We are both in love with other people
who do not love us.
But I follow this small bliss
wherever it wanders
on these sunrise drives

through our postage stamp town
where everyone wakes up
hours before dawn to go to work
at making rich men who do not live here richer.
As we pass by the house where I grew up,
he slows the car, knows
I am fascinated by the colors
the new owners have chosen
for the window treatments,
the lilies planted in the yard.
We park at the high school,
cross the street hand in hand
to the cemetery.
He shows me the place
where his grandfather lives now,
the family plot
where the letters of his own last name
shimmer in the morning sun.
There are no words for the feeling
that settles between my ribs,
that perches there like hope
and despair all at once,
his arm wrapped
around my waist,
lips warm and still against my ear
in the pale, streaming light.

At 7pm

You board a plane to Las Vegas
bound for a supporting role in a wedding
you do not believe has anything to do with love.
Earlier, we'd made love on an old mattress
on the floor of your best friend's apartment,
the hard shell of your suitcase banging
into my knee, your mouth wet
with the harsh scrape of my name.
There was little romance in it,
only the frenzied unleashing
of the not-knowing,
the possibility of unhappy endings, cutthroat desire.
I do not love you.
Or, rather, I love you
as I would love a deck of cards
while waiting for a train or a bus.
Our goodbyes fly across a crowded room
like small white birds.
At the ticket counter,
you kiss me with lips smooth as Cary Grant.
In the car, the radio plays songs to name
every sort of love
that does not bloom
in my heart for you,
and the long white lines of the road,
like dark-haired college boys
with bodies pale as ghosts,
take me home to bed.

Letting Go

Up in the hayloft of his grandfather's old red barn,
the tin roof shakes with every strike of the storm,
and we can feel the thunder deep in our chests
rattling our hearts inside their bony cages.
George Strait is on the radio singing
about love and lonesome old roads.
This time, we take it slow
and lazy as the Sunday rain—
him underneath, bare-chested,
and me
in his blue flannel shirt
that flares like a waterfall over my hips.
When he starts to shake, it is not from the cold.
In the lantern-light, he trusts me enough
to let me see his brokenness.
My name and God's pour from him like steam,
his lips hot as an iron brand on my collarbone.
In the morning, the barn and the farmhouse
and the cows and horses and sheep
will be sold,
the acres of fertile land that surround us
parceled and auctioned off.
We have seen the signs all over town,
lining the highway, the sight of them alone
enough to tighten his hands
on the steering wheel
as we speed together
down the unlined road,
silos rising in the distance
like obelisks against the sagging, gray sky.
I imagine the creek, already swollen,
has swallowed the rocks
where he and his cousins
would sit for hours, a bunch of rowdy boys,

feet bare and pants rolled past their ankles,
lures bobbing in the muddy water
until their grandmother called them up for supper.
Even the barn, burned once to the ground
and rebuilt—where he made forts
out of hay bales and empty crates
stacked clear up to the rafters
where he could finally see the world
like a king on his throne, invincible in his tower—
shudders and creaks in the rough arms of the wind
as though it might fall to pieces.
But someday. Not now. For now, it holds on
like a good, faithful woman.
Below, the horses snort and stamp in their stalls,
as restless as me when he slips his hands
down my back, wrestles me to the floor.
I let him, only because I know
how powerless he feels most of the time,
and how boys like him will fall in love
with the world,
like fools,
when it is not easily conquered.

Bellwether

The party, with its middle-aged DJ, became so boring
that we retreated up the back staircase, two lost children
laughing and clutching one another
in the dark,
our faces splashed
with bright blue patches of neon light
thrown through the windows
from the bar next door.
Half-drunk, we stumbled into the room
where the coats and scarves
and gloves of guests
lay scattered on the wide bed.
Kissing my neck, you asked, "Want to?"
as if I could say no to you.
No on this—
our first time together in New York,
snow heavy, wet and glistening
up and down the avenues
like a soft blanket of *shhhh...*
Not while you radiated heat
like a million summer suns, the sweet,
mint-tinged pulse of your breath
on my skin, teasing my thighs apart.
My pale body shimmering
like Van Gogh's watery stars; your hands hot stones
working at knots, untying me.
No words for this undoing, this animal bliss.
We took what we wanted from one another,
kisses red as sieves of wine,
the fine golden things we promised,
our ring fingers curled together
in the dark among the coats and scarves and gloves
still damp and shapeless, empty of curve and of breath,
waiting for something warm and solid to slip inside,
waiting for something to cling to.

If You Ever Leave Me, I'll Kill You...

he says and removes one bullet
from his last box of the season,
sets it on the table between us. A dare.
Silence, thick and red, coats my tongue.
Blood pools in the backyard, below
the meaty carcass of the doe he shot that morning.
She hangs next to the woodpile
by her hind legs from the lowest branch
of the sycamore I begged him
not to cut down the year before.
As evening closes in, crows gather
to tear at her intestines curled
like a length of black rope on the ground.
He has started to sleep with his gun;
and that single bullet, christened
with my name, rests like an omen
in the chamber.
In the morning, I dress and go to work like nothing
is different, as though I am not an animal
being watched through the trees
by a hunter who can smell me on the wind
and knows every blessed trick
to lure me out of hiding, who sees
every desperate move I will make
long before I think to make it.

Remains

The sidewalk is ice under our feet, and we shiver
in the wind as you pass me a cigarette
and your lighter. I take a quick drag.
Smoke numbs my tongue, my lips.
Side by side, we flick ashes into the
wet belly of the night. Blocks away,
we can hear the clang and rattle
of the garbage truck as it makes its rounds, swallowing
whatever it is offered by the hands of men
who will continue to take it for granted
until the day it draws blood
or wrestles away a limb. Until something vital
goes missing. Because I am not
in love with you, I can appreciate
the way your mouth curls around the clipped
syllables of her name, the girl who left you.
Beside me, you shift your weight from foot to foot,
eyes darting from my face to the horizon,
to the place where the moon would be
if she weren't off hiding in shadows,
if this were a different time of month.
To anyone passing by, we could be just two kids
under the streetlights, hoods pulled up,
cherries aglow with each inhale, the soft white horses
of our breath galloping around us.
Really, what do we know about loss?
I feel fourteen again when you ask
how I've been, and all I can do is sigh
his name and a list of things I regret
that sound like a stack of unpaid bills
or a pile of dirty laundry I can't bring myself
to sort through. When you open the door
of your home to me, there is an endless loop
of sad songs pouring from the stereo.

I want to make dinner for you and tuck you
into bed. Instead, you bring me a glass of sweet tea
and laugh about the fact that you have no TV
to watch because she didn't pay the bill
before she split, and for weeks the mailbox
has sat as empty as a mouth hungry for
the porkchops she cooked or the kinds of kisses
that polite folks never talk about in public.
And I get it. All of it. I want to throw it
out onto the curb to be swept up
and away like old newspapers, apple cores,
stale milk and the curling, blackening
skins of potatoes. The garbage truck
turns onto your street as we hug goodbye
and I walk down the block to my car.
The men laugh and carry on, heft trash bins
up over their heads like Heisman trophies,
toss each empty can back to the curb.
Some fall, tumble and roll into the shallow
maw of the gutter where I imagine
they will lie and count the long, desolate hours
until they are filled again, until they
can stand again on their own.

Layover, Dallas/Fort Worth

Around us—
lemon pledge, orange glow—
a dense cloud of citrus
cancels out the soft song of my perfume,
the tang of your aftershave,
our sweat as you lift and push me
against the lowest shelf of the janitor's closet.
And we forget for a moment
our humanness,
minds blotting out the mysterious wet spots
under our shoes,
broken brooms piled in a corner
like kindling.
We forget the people in the hall,
less than fifty feet away,
who rush by with briefcases, with phones
or travel mugs filled with coffee.
Human things.
Behind the thin barrier of the unlocked door,
they stampede like cattle in a slaughterhouse.
But here, in our dark pasture, the moon
is a flickering bulb overhead.
The light cord swings back and forth,
casts a long black shadow
like the wings of a horned owl
fanned across your face.

The crease in your jeans flattens
against me as you move,
like an animal, teeth buried in me,
muscles wound tight and galloping
toward a starry sky of blessed oblivion.
Long tongues of fire sweep like rivers
under my skin, and the fish have learned
to speak your name in many languages.
In whispers, they beg you to come
and drink.

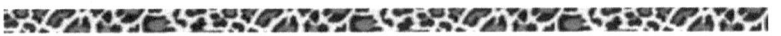

Romancing the Astronomer

He comes alive like a bright asterisk
in the dreary sentence of a country back road
the tails of fireflies like meteors
hurtling through the space between us,

arms like white lilies blooming
from the shadows of his black t-shirt,
his lips a tidal wave
ready to come crashing down on mine.

In the lap of July
his sharpness startles me awake.

It begins to rain
just minutes past midnight.

With his clean-shaven
all-American face tilted to the sky
he tells me
that even the sun will fail us one day
will become a plume of flame
will engulf and melt everything

will burn
our solar system
to ash
our very molecules, the dust of our skins
will meld with comets
carried off into galaxies beyond
our knowing.

There is a pocket map of New Mexico
folded into his wallet
photos of Area 51.

He is in love with the sky
and what falls from it.

His phone comes alive in his pocket
the bells and whistles of our world
pulling him back under
the heavy blanket of the here and now.

He tells me later
that he does not believe in God
or miracles
or much of anything anymore,

and when he comes to my bed
swathed in his robe of numbers and puzzles
his confessions of a life he wants to leave behind,
I kiss him with fervor and linger
in the dark rectories of his mind,

press my naked body
like a memory of constellations
against the backs of his eyelids

hoping to

burn away the cruel edges of the starless night
that surround him
like a column of fire

wholly and impossibly kind.

Gravity

Years ago, I was twenty
pressed up against the old dented washing machine
in that dank little basement room
with some boy's lips sucking
the flesh of my neck hard enough
to leave bruises in the shape of small storm clouds.
My first wild moment stretched
hours past midnight
into the speckled October dawn.
I was becoming a very different animal
shaped out of earthen mud and clay
by the trembling hands of a young and clumsy god—
full of blood and magic as it grappled
with the cosmic weight of a woman's first desire.
In my girlhood bed, I was divided in the neon light,
a star pulling herself into being.
His body, the night sky—
the first to know me, to feel the flush
of my heat on his upturned face,
my eyes drawing him in and in,
two long-lashed galaxies thick and dark
with enough gravity
to send him spinning.

At the Motel 6

With its smoke-laced sheets,
its ghosts kicking inside the walls
like the limbs of unwanted children,
Gideon Bible crushed
unread in one corner
of an empty drawer
next to a dead TV remote.
Our sweaters mingle
in a careless heap
over the back of the desk chair,
ruddy lamplight
cascades like lava
over the smooth white
peaks of our legs.

You pour two cups of coffee
black and boundless
as a witch's scrying mirror.

You call me
your Pele, your maiden of fire, your sweet little flame.

Your body a vessel
tattooed with the shivery lines
of uncertain futures, red and fine
as strings of fate
carried to term
or sacrificed
in some back alley
in the dead of night.

You press the knife
of your open palm
to my cheek
and tell me to breathe, keep breathing
this won't hurt
for long.

Flash Point

(noun) 1. As in physical chemistry, the lowest temperature at which a volatile liquid in a specified apparatus will give off sufficient vapor to ignite momentarily upon application of flame. 2. A critical point or stage at which something or someone suddenly causes or creates some significant action. 3. A critical situation or area having the potential of erupting in sudden violence.

The radio DJ working graveyard shift
at the local country station tells us
this is the coldest November night
on record in ten years. It is
another night parked in the field, tucked
into the back of your car. The cows have all been
called home. We are left as alone as Jesus
on Calvary Hill, clinging to the golden apple
of youth, our blessed invincibility.

In the temple of the sky,
Orion takes his aim,
silver bow drawn, pointed
toward the earth.
Your breath comes
in short gasps, as though you already bear
the cross of an arrow
in the space between your ribs.

Earlier, you told me
about your dream,
about the flames that licked
at your face, surrounded
and swallowed you whole,
how you woke drenched in sweat
and could still feel the burning
like hellfire, the sensation of your skin
melting, sliding off the bone.

For hours, you paced the house,
checking and double-checking
the latches on windows to be sure
they did not stick, exchanging
batteries in smoke detectors.
Finally, unable to sleep, you dialed
my number and your voice
cracked and shook
like dry husks of corn
in the wind when you said,

*I need to get out
of this goddamn house.*

Beneath you, I cry out
at the same moment as the whistle
of the midnight train as it roars by,
the length of it measuring out hours
like bolts of cloth, slicing
the night neatly in two.

Like a man with something to prove,
your muscles clench and you go still,
fighting back the heat that rises
under your skin with everything you have.

You lean in to kiss me, deep
as the river and refuse to come
up for air as the train thunders on
through the cleft of the countryside
steady as a racing heartbeat
to God knows where,

as if this is all the evidence you will ever need,
the precious assurance that you
can outlast anything.

Summer, One Year Later

When I drag the green camp chair from the shed,
unfold and anchor it on the hillside that overlooks the field
where families of deer push their way
through the deep rows of corn, the sun has already sunk low
behind the blue veils of mountains,
the horizon a skinny ribbon of red
tied across the darkness,
lit up like a roadside flare.
Sometimes, nobody comes.
Gunshots echo across the valley
from the range just a mile up the road.
A breeze from the north carries the smell
of burning charcoal,
firewood, seared meat.
Somewhere, children are laughing,
and the trees shiver with joy.
Country music pours from a radio,
a dog barks.
Down by the river, fireworks pop and whine,
their fingers of white light
rising and reaching,
raking across the freckled cheek of the night sky.
In high school, I read that the stars
in our sky are long dead. We see only echoes.
Nothing lasts.
Eventually, I stopped wishing for things.

Tonight is the kind of night made
for the kind of girls who still believe
in the perpetual heat of the sun,
the thrill of first kisses,
promises as big and dreamy as the silver sliver of moon
balanced on a wooden fencepost.
I have never been a girl who is good
with endings, the same song
always on repeat until I can sing each word in my sleep.
So, tonight, I hold your name like a wish
on the tip of my tongue and wait
at the mouth of these woods
like a lost hiker
for something—anything—to pass by
that might be worthy of carrying you.

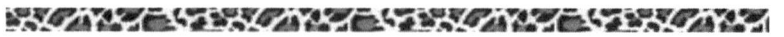

An Inventory of Lost Things

My car keys,
my virginity,
a silver lighter, a pack of cigarettes,
a pair of lacy black panties
in the backseat of a blue Chevrolet,
one husband,
a bottle of perfume,
a love letter from a dead boyfriend
that still carries the sweet echo of his cologne,
countless notebooks full
of brilliant poems,
my father,
my father's red handkerchief,
my mother's gold ring,
my inhibitions,
my glasses
in an airport bathroom,
your phone number,
a velvet bag of guitar picks,
a Joan Jett CD,
the will to live,
the complete poems of Sylvia Plath,
a tube of perfect, pink lipstick,
a contact lens on a bus in San Pedro,
a lover in Portland,
a pack of gum
on a New York City subway train,
a chance to say goodbye,
a chance to say I love you,
eighty pounds of fat,
my fear of crowded places,

two dogs to some nameless sickness
and once
a pet turtle,
the only photo of you and I
in existence,
a fistful of laundry quarters,
my favorite childhood toy,
those sweet words you whispered
into my ear
when you thought I was sleeping,
all my colored socks,
my favorite pen,
a pair of black cowboy boots

and my heart,
my goddamn heart.

What She Doesn't Know

After months of coaxing, I finally find myself
in the immaculate kitchen of his mother's
stonefaced house on the affluent side of town
where the front yards are all filled
with white Christmas lights and nativities,
and the smell of fabric softener
wafts up from the dryer vents.
There is no neighborhood watch;
instead, there are spotlights aimed
like the star of Bethlehem at every front door.

She is beautiful, his mother, even if she
tries too hard, hair gathered onto her head
in an elegant style that begins to tumble loose
from its small army of bobby pins
to curl against her cheeks as she serves us dinner,
slides a helping of lemon-basil chicken
and brown rice onto my plate. She calls me honey,
tells me I have lovely eyes.

I suspect that I may be falling in love
with this woman when she pours a glass
of white wine for me without asking,
places the bottle within easy reach.
She settles into her chair, finally,
at the head of the table, exhausted
but regal as a Madonna in her
sugarplum gown, the string
of pearls at her throat swallowing the light
from the forest of white candles
she has planted and lit
on every flat surface
in the room.

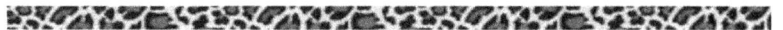

She smiles the slow smile of the pleasantly drunk
and tells me how wonderful it is
to have another woman in the house
for a change. With a clumsy flap of her napkin,
she says she wants to read my poetry

and for a moment I feel almost evil,
imagining how shocked she would be
to discover just how many of those poems
are about me fucking her shy, apple-cheeked
twenty year-old son
in the backseat of his car,
miles of verse to commemorate
my naked body unraveling in his hands
like a knitted sweater.

So, instead, my gift to her is to smile and pour
myself another glass of wine, to summon
the kindest, softest words I know
like Bing Crosby crooning from the stereo
about dreams of snow as pure and white
as her son's perfect smile,
to tell her that these poems
are not for her.

Gathering Storm

Somewhere in the ruddy sandscape
of the Mojave Desert, a tire fails
and we rumble to a stop
at the side of the road.
A mad sun scorches asphalt,
bakes the leather interior of our rental
as we climb out into the heat.
Sweat covers his bare back in a glaze
as he works, pools in the narrow canyon
where my breasts meet
beneath the thin cotton
of his t-shirt that I'm wearing.
He eases the shredded tire to the ground,
slides the new one into place, simple
and effortless as his hand finding its way back
into mine after years apart.
I open a bottle of lukewarm water
and drink, greedy as a mountain cat,
as if this will be the last time.
Speckled lizards scurry over the ground
at my feet; I tower over their kingdom
of sun-split rocks like an ivory-skinned princess,
and suddenly he is there, plundering the depths
of his rucksack to lather the exposed
curve of my shoulders, my bare white arms
with sunscreen.
He touches his dry lips to my neck,
a gift, precious as water.
"Never drive into the desert without a spare," he says.
The smile that curves his lips is an echo
of the bow my father used to hunt whitetail deer
in the green, wild forests back east.

Here, the vultures circle overhead
like hooded messengers and cast shadows
across the bright planes of our faces.
Here, it is early afternoon, and the sun still
rides high, a golden chariot dashing apart
what few clouds stagger on the horizon,
stealing away
even the faintest hope for rain
while the storm inside of me gathers
and shakes.

Amber Decker is a poet from West Virginia who has never, despite Hollywood's colorful depictions of her Appalachian roots, had sex with any relatives or animals, nor has she ever cannibalized anyone who has taken a...wrong turn. She has worn many hats—disgruntled delivery girl, security dispatcher, warehouse drone, rodeo princess, massage therapist but she always comes back to poetry on nights when the moon is full and her heart (or her glass) is half-empty. Amber is in love with love. She's the kind of girl who leaves the house in the middle of the night to go driving with all four windows wound down and the radio cranked up, "just to think." She is a firm believer in the undeniable power of really awesome, world-shattering sex. And hot wings. Those are nice, too.

A Million Thank Yous:

Todd & Julie & Matt, of course, of course.

Linda...my best friend, my sister, my shining star. I love you.

Justin Rosenwald and beautiful wife Nicole for allowing your garage to be my drunken sanctuary.

West Virginia Writers, Inc.

Morgantown Poets.

Mike Harsh...an amazing educator. I will always choose to "be bold" because of you.

My specials: Kendall & Christinia Bell, Taylor Emily Copeland, Stefanie Meade, April Johnson, Joshua Robinson, Allie Marini Batts, Larissa Nash, Ginger Hamilton, Robbie Newcome, Susan Rich, Kelli Russell Agodon, Rick Lupert, Walter Rhulmann, Carolee Bartel and Susan Sheppard.

The poem, "Remains", in this book is lovingly dedicated to Joey Jackson who, in the end, got the girl. I'm glad we had that talk.

www.ingramcontent.com/pod-product-compliance
Lightning Source LLC
Chambersburg PA
CBHW071759040426
42446CB00012B/2634